TO

_____

DATE

_____

Trusting God When You Have Cancer

HELP AND HOPE FOR THE ROAD AHEAD

JERRY COOK & RON PINKSTON

PHOTOGRAPHY BY NANCY J. LOCKE

HARVEST HOUSE PUBLISHERS

EUGENE, OREGON

To my Lord and Savior, Jesus Christ

who promised me that I would be well and kept His promise, as always

To my beloved wife, Susan, and children David, Sarah, and Joshua

To my indispensible helpers Mom, Dan, Kim, and Lisa

To my great friends Jerry, Jim, and Wil

To the staff and congregation of East Bay Fellowship

Ron

Trusting God When You Have Cancer

Text Copyright © 2009 by Jerry Cook and Ron Pinkston. Artwork © Nancy J. Locke, LLC
Licensed by The Knight Agency, Inc.

Published by Harvest House Publishers

Eugene, Oregon 97402

www.harvesthousepublishers.com

ISBN 978-0-7369-2519-8

All photographs were taken in Michigan, including: Lake Superior, Lake Huron, Lake Superior State
Forest, Hiawatha National Forest, Pictured Rocks National Lakeshore, Tahquamenon Falls State Park,
and the photographer's land.

Design and production by Koechel Peterson & Associates, Inc., Minneapolis, Minnesota

Scripture quotations are taken from the HOLY BIBLE, NEW INTERNATIONAL VERSION®. NIV®.
Copyright©1973, 1978, 1984 by the International Bible Society. Used by permission of Zondervan. All
rights reserved. Verses marked NKJV are taken from the New King James Version. Copyright © 1982
by Thomas Nelson, Inc. Used by permission. All rights reserved.

Harvest House Publishers has made every effort to trace the ownership of all poems and quotes. In the
event of a question arising from the use of a poem or quote, we regret any error made and will be pleased
to make the necessary correction in future editions of this book.

Printed in China

09 10 11 12 13 14 15 / LP / 10 9 8 7 6 5 4 3 2 1

To Christi, Dan, Jamie, Lady J, Meg, Sandar and Carmen,
whose constant love gave me hope;
and to Barbara, my companion, my friend, my hero.
Jerry

CONTENTS

I HAD RECOVERED enough from surgery to begin chemotherapy for colon cancer. The past month had been a nightmare. Then Ron called to tell me his doctors had found a tumor and the biopsy had shown it was cancerous. He would begin chemo in two weeks.

I was devastated. Ron and I had been close friends for many years. That he would be going through what I was experiencing was almost overwhelming to me. Then I thought we could share the journey. I told him I would write a letter during each of my chemo treatments. The idea was to walk along the road together and talk. Convey our thoughts, emotions, and fears...all the stuff that goes into these kinds of things. I hoped our correspondence would encourage him. Little did I know the healing it would bring to me as well.

This brief book contains excerpts from those letters. It is our hope that our correspondence will lighten your journey and give you hope. Perhaps our letters will encourage you to share the road with someone you love. We also desire that these exchanges illustrate a healthy, deep friendship between two men who love God, their families, and each other in a world where such relationships are far too rare.

The letters do not follow in the order of their writing, but rather have been chosen as some that meant a great deal to us at the time. All eighteen of my letters can be seen at www.jerrycook.org. Just click on "cancer."

CHAPTER ONE

FINDING A FRIEND

A friend loves at all times,

and a brother

is born for adversity.

PROVERBS 17:17

ONE OF THE MOST important things, when cancer strikes, is to find a friend to walk through the experience with you. And it is especially helpful if you can find someone who is either experiencing cancer at the same time or has experienced it in the past—in other words, someone who can really relate to what you're going through.

Jerry and I had been friends for years. But this new and horrible challenge took our friendship to another level. It provided comfort no one else could give us in quite the same way. It still does.

Dear Jerry,

I can't tell you how much it means to me to have you ahead of me on the same road. On the one hand, I'm so sorry you have to experience this. I wish it were just me. On the other hand, I can't think of anyone else in the world I'd rather follow down any road—especially this one.

My diagnosis started with a lot of pain. I hurt so much I decided to go to a chiropractor for the first time in my life. The more the chiropractor worked on me, the worse the pain got. Eventually, she said I should see my primary physician as soon as possible. I think it's fair to say her advice saved my life.

At first my primary physician thought I had an ulcer, but when the prescribed medications didn't seem to be working, he ordered a CAT scan and got me in the next day to get it done. That afternoon, the news came back that I had a tumor in my abdomen that was probably lymphoma. It all happened so fast I hardly had time to react. One minute I was joking with friends about the fact that my ulcer couldn't be caused by stress and the next minute I was staring cancer in its ugly, distorted face.

Like you, I didn't know what to feel. All I could think about were the people I love. What would my wife do without me? How would my children and grandchildren feel about God and life? Questions like those swirled around in my head like a whirlpool and rushed over the edge like the roaring waters of Niagara Falls.

But very quickly I came across a passage in the Bible that comforted my heart. I knew the Lord was comforting me and telling me He would send this enemy home overwhelmed by the things we would see God do. One of the first signs confirming that truth was your desire to send me a letter every week. What an expression of grace that someone I love so much would make such an incredible offer out of the blue!

Keep me in your rearview mirror. I'm right behind you all the way. Your friendship means more to me than you can possibly know in this season.

Your friend forever,
Ron

ONE MINUTE I WAS JOKING WITH FRIENDS ABOUT THE FACT THAT MY ULCER COULDN'T BE CAUSED BY STRESS AND THE NEXT MINUTE I WAS STARING CANCER IN ITS UGLY, DISTORTED FACE.

FINDING A FRIEND

Nearly everyone knows someone who's been through cancer, which sadly means you probably do too. Take advantage of that sadness and turn it into comfort by mining the ore of friendship. Doing that will help you in ways you can't even imagine right now. It will help you talk about things you want to hide from, provide a vantage point you can't yet see, and strengthen you when weakness comes in like a flood.

One of the great possibilities of this season of your life, or the life of your loved one, is newfound and deepened friendships. Go after them. The difference they will make in your life may make you want to write a book someday.

Dear friend, I pray that you may enjoy

good health and that all may go well with you.

3 JOHN 2

CHAPTER TWO

DAYS OF DENIAL

Denial is the psychological process by which human beings protect themselves from things which threaten them.

SOMETIMES DENIAL can be a healthy thing. In the life of a cancer patient, it can be the difference between wanting to give up and wanting to live another day.

In this chapter, I contemplate thoughts Jerry has previously shared with me about this concept of denial. We recognize there is a price to pay. But in our case, it's a price worth paying. For us, a little more pain and/or nausea as the result of a good time is a fair exchange.

Obviously, denial for any substantial length of time can be dangerous. Anyone with any sensibility at all knows that, but don't be afraid to indulge yourself. Don't be afraid to take a day off from your sickness. Go out to dinner. Go fishing. Do whatever it is you did when you were having fun before all of this started.

Dear Jerry,

I laughed 'til I cried when I read about your "denial day." Thank you for giving me the freedom to live a day without cancer—at least in my mind. I shared this concept with Susan, and we laughed together and made plans for our day of denial.

It makes so much sense. No matter what the statistical possibilities of recovery are, cancer has a hopeless tag attached to it. It can eat away at your mental health as fast as it can destroy your body. I've always believed in a day of rest. So, when you brought this up, it resonated throughout my being like a Seattle breeze on a hot California day!

As I considered this day of denial, I found myself enjoying the refocus. I savored each detail as I planned my day. I thought to myself, I'm tired of eating tomato soup. I'm tired of getting out of bed only to walk to the living room and eventually return to my bed again. I felt as though I were living in the movie What About Bob? And you gave me a prescription to take a day off from myself!

Speaking of prescriptions, I could really identify with your lament about medications. I'm not taking as many as you, but on the basis of recommendations from my nutritional team, I'm definitely taking at least 16 pills (and other concoctions) on a daily basis. I might even take a day off from them, or at least the ones not absolutely necessary.

Oh, and one more thing...no doctors and no nurses are going on my day of denial. I really value what they do for me, but they don't belong in my imagination.

Anyway, God bless you and your brilliant mind. Over the years, God has used you countless times to plant a new and fertile concept in my brain. The Day of Denial (you could call it "rest" or "Sabbath") has to be one of the best.

I deeply love you, my friend. And I agree—we will get through this together.

Your friend in the rearview mirror,
Ron

I'M TIRED OF GETTING

OUT OF BED ONLY

TO WALK TO THE

LIVING ROOM AND

EVENTUALLY RETURN

TO MY BED AGAIN.

DAYS OF DENIAL

You are in charge of your life. No doctor or nurse or statistician can determine your happiness for today. No one else is responsible for your choices. Don't be afraid to make decisions that give you an emotional break.

None of us really knows how many days we have left in this life. Taking one of them as a day of rest from the battle might end up being one of the best decisions you make. It will help clear your head and heart and help you put things in their proper perspective. It's kind of like pushing the reset button on electronic devices. Go ahead...push it!

[Jesus said,] "Come with me by yourselves
to a quiet place and get some rest."

MARK 6:31

CHAPTER THREE

NEW SENSATIONS

To you it seems like a mess, but to me, I see a perfect pattern emerging and growing and alive—

a living fractal.

WILLIAM P. YOUNG

ONE OF THE FIRST doses of reality takes place when chemotherapy begins to change your physical and chemical makeup. For most people it starts gradually, involving relatively minor things like nausea, tingling, pain in the extremities, light-headedness, or just a general sense of weirdness.

Those sensations signal a new season. Now you're not just battling the disease but the symptoms of the poison placed in your system to fight the disease. It's the ultimate paradox, a complete irony.

Feelings stronger than intellect—emotional and physical—can have overriding power. They can blow out the circuits, crash the hard drive, and destroy what is eminently logical on a normal day…if you're unprepared for them.

Understanding new sensations as a good thing is helped by knowing they're coming in advance—nothing like a little preparation to avoid a lot of perspiration. When you know what sensations may be on the horizon, it makes their arrival much more tolerable, a living fractal.

Dear Jerry,

I definitely related to your description of new sensations you experienced in chemotherapy. The nurses told me I would likely get drowsy from the medication they gave me to counteract the chemo, but I didn't. Instead, I listened to my iPod incessantly. Music was soothing to my soul and a healthy distraction from the knowledge that I was being intentionally poisoned—and the feelings that accompanied that poisoning.

Thankfully, my bouts with nausea have been limited. But I did have a good one recently. I was supposed to get a colonoscopy (something every man my age should do), but I couldn't hold down the formula they want you to drink the night before the procedure. I went to bed and asked Susan to call the next day to let them know there's no way I can do that until I'm done with all this chemo stuff.

I have noticed some of the sensations you talked about starting to happen, especially an hour or two after it's over. I have to take antinausea pills two or three times a day. In fact, because of the steroids, I can't sleep without those pills. I tried for a few nights, but I just ended up lying awake most of those nights filled with endless inspirations for changing the world. Talk about a sensation. I was e-mailing people at 1:00 and 2:00 in the morning about things I was sure were going to make the entire world more efficient.

Finally I realized, with Susan's help, that these sleepless nights were chemically induced rather than spiritually inspired. I got on the antinausea meds and found restless but stable sleep.

I can tell you honestly that your letters are an antidote for me. Every time I read one, I get good sensations inside. Please keep them coming. I look forward to them like a hound dog looks forward to the scent of a fox. Talk to you soon.

Your friend in the rearview mirror,
Ron

MUSIC WAS SOOTHING TO MY SOUL AND A HEALTHY DISTRACTION FROM THE KNOWLEDGE THAT I WAS BEING INTENTIONALLY POISONED.

NEW SENSATIONS

Sorting out new physical and emotional sensations can seem like standing in the middle of a maze with no sense of direction or smell. Up can seem down and down can seem up. You can be cruising along with what feels like a normal day when all of a sudden the floor drops out.

The key is getting help from someone who has experienced those sensations. Not only will you feel better about what you're feeling, you will probably find yourself laughing as you hear the other person's descriptions of those feelings.

Here's the point. Don't be afraid of the new sensations you are experiencing. They are a normal part of the journey.

When you pass through the waters,
I will be with you;
and when you pass through the rivers,
they will not sweep over you.

ISAIAH 43:2

CHAPTER FOUR

GRATITUDE

We're not joyful

and then we become

grateful—

we're grateful and

that makes us joyful.

BRENNEN MANNING

ONE OF THE MOST POWERFUL and helpful of all human emotions is gratitude. And the hardest time to find it is when our world reaches its darkest hours. Yet that is when we need gratitude the most.

In the same way chemotherapy kills the rampant cells destroying our bodies, gratitude is a God-designed antidote to the ravages of depression, anger, grief, and other potentially self-destructive emotions common to our battle with cancer. Gratitude suffocates those negative emotions with positive ones.

In this letter I talk about the discovery of gratitude in the midst of pain and suffering and the joy of sharing that discovery. It's like finding water in the desert. It must be what the forty-niners felt when they discovered gold in the midst of their bone-tired efforts.

17

Dear Jerry,

I know what you mean by "deep peace and gratitude." I've felt it too, even though it seems more than a little strange to feel grateful in the middle of this milieu.

Like you, I've been overwhelmed by that deep awareness that God didn't give this cancer to me, that in fact He loves me more than I am able to comprehend. I've never felt more like a beloved child than I do now. And feeling childlike is something I haven't felt in a long time.

Another part of my gratitude comes from the many indirect expressions of love coming through messengers like you. It seems that every day someone tells me how much they love me in a card, an e-mail, a phone call, or a live conversation. It is humbling to know how much we really are loved. And it makes my heart swell with gratitude toward my wife, my children, my friends, and the many acquaintances who have offered to help in some way.

What makes it all so amazing is that I feel this gratitude in the most ironic moment of life. I should be bitter, angry, and closed up inside, but this trial has put everything in perspective and given me a fresh look at God and everyone around me.

Thanksgiving will never just be a holiday for me again. I announced my illness to my extended family on Thanksgiving Day. Since that time, I have never felt closer to everyone I love than I do now. Funny—I'm being poisoned on the inside by chemo but being detoxified in my soul by gratitude. All I can say is, "Keep it coming, Lord!"

Right behind your bumper…and grateful to be there,
Ron

I SHOULD BE BITTER, ANGRY, AND CLOSED UP INSIDE, BUT THIS TRIAL HAS PUT EVERYTHING IN PERSPECTIVE AND GIVEN ME A FRESH LOOK AT GOD AND EVERYONE AROUND ME.

Be joyful always...
give thanks in all circumstances.

1 THESSALONIANS 5:16,18

GRATITUDE

Every day has a fork in the road. We can choose to travel down the road of self-pity, self-introspection, or self-absorption. The problem is that fork always leads to a dead end. It leaves us weary, discouraged, and out of options because we were never meant to live life on our own. And we certainly don't have all the answers.

On the other hand, we can choose gratitude. Admittedly, this is the road less traveled. But then, that means a smoother ride—less bumps, chuckholes, and loose debris. This road always leads to somewhere better than where we are. It lifts us out of the mundane and invites us into the Divine.

Strangely, if we don't make the choice, it will be made for us by the circumstances. Most of us are like cars with our wheels out of alignment. We automatically drift toward bitterness. Gratitude realigns our souls and keeps us on the right road.

CHAPTER FIVE

LAUGHTER

Research has shown health benefits of laughter ranging from strengthening the immune system to reducing food cravings to increasing one's threshold for pain.

ELIZABETH SCOTT, M.S.

IT'S HARD TO LAUGH in the midst of a storm. The elements are raging, demanding that our emotions go along for the ride. Similar to being on a roller coaster, if you do laugh it can sometimes feel a little hysterical.

But laughter is a proven form of medicine. More than 3000 years ago, a very wise man said, "A merry heart does good like a medicine" (Proverbs 17:22). Now we have scientific facts to prove it.

One of the best things you can do to ride out this storm called cancer is to find things that make you laugh and pursue them. Watch a funny movie. Talk to friends who make you laugh. Go to a comedy show. Don't be afraid. You won't break anything.

Dear Jerry,

What a great idea—make a commitment to laughter! I couldn't agree more. And like you, people have started sending me humorous cards, videos, and e-mails. I love it. Every time I laugh (even though sometimes it hurts physically), paradoxically the pain subsides. It's like a little extra shot of mental morphine.

Something you said in your letter actually got me laughing. It was when you said the doctors and nurses told you the sicker you got the better the chemo was working. Or, in your words, "The worse you feel, the better it is." Well, we must both be doing incredibly well, then, because I've had plenty of worse days in the poison cell.

It's funny how even something like that can create a chuckle. When you're this far down in the barrel, everything looks up. I can see the irony in almost everything. I've had my share of depression. I've had my share of pain. I've had my share of bouts with confusion. It's time for a little humor. I'm ready.

But it's not just slapstick, frivolous humor I'm committing myself to. It is also the simple pleasures of life. You talked about fixing up your new house as "pure fun." For me, pure fun consists of conversations with my wife, walks with my son, short meetings with staff members in my home, and visits from friends who have come a long distance to see me. Those fundamental points of relationship bring great joy to my heart and soothe my battered body and soul.

Thanks for reminding me how important laughter is. I'm committing with you to looking for the humor in each day and being careful to not take myself or my condition too seriously. They say that after a broken bone heals, it is actually stronger than the original version at the point of the break. Together, I'm sure we will come out of this trial with seriously strengthened funny bones!

Laughing as I look for you in the mirror,
Ron

IT'S FUNNY HOW EVEN SOMETHING LIKE THAT CAN CREATE A CHUCKLE. WHEN YOU'RE THIS FAR DOWN IN THE BARREL, EVERYTHING LOOKS UP.

LAUGHTER

Why don't some of us laugh more? Sometimes it's a hangover from our family of origin where things weren't that funny on a daily basis. Sometimes it's the grind of our work schedule. Sometimes it is the gravity of the illness we're standing in front of, bringing us face-to-face with our mortality.

Whatever it is doesn't matter. We know the indisputable value of laughter and joy. In the same way we take the medicine prescribed for us by our oncologist, we must take the biblical prescription of a merry heart.

On the previous page, you heard about the commitment Jerry and I made together. Why not join us? Make a commitment today to those things that bring joy to your heart. Often the people around us are afraid to make jokes because of our situation. Let people know you want to laugh. They'll help you get well faster!

A cheerful heart is good medicine.

PROVERBS 17:22

CHAPTER SIX

Pain

> The *I* in illness is isolation, and the crucial letters in wellness are *we*.
>
> AUTHOR UNKNOWN

THERE IS NO WAY to have a painless battle with cancer. Pain always lurks in the background when we're awake or asleep. At times, it marches in and blatantly demands our time and exhausts our already depleted energy.

Dealing with pain has a great deal to do with how we think and what license we give to our emotions. In this letter I describe a particularly difficult time near the end of my chemo treatment as I am struggling to get stable enough to start radiation.

Dear Ron,

I am learning more about separating my physical situation from my emotions. It must not, nor can it be, separated completely. We cannot live a fractured life. But we must not let the physical determine or control the emotional and spiritual.

An interesting development is my attitude towards pain. Pain connected directly with the cancer and therefore lethal in its implications is much less tolerable, though it may be less intense. Pain that is not lethal—cramps, the pelvic fractures, chemo-associated aches, etc.—may be much greater in intensity but much more easily tolerated and managed. In fact, I am tending to disregard what I consider nonlethal pain. For example, the fractures... My back and hip hurt constantly and so intensely that I seldom get more than three hours' relief from the pain pills, day or night. But because this pain will not kill me, I don't take it very seriously. I must force myself to remember that pain is a system alert and should not be ignored or disrespected—lethal or not.

I'm not sure what all this means. I do know I can easily overlook Barb's feelings. My pain is of great concern to her. She feels it deeply and wants to do something about it, when there really is nothing more to do. She tries to keep me from doing anything that hurts, when to me pain is a given. I find myself, disappointingly, becoming impatient with her concerns.

I know how much I want to fix any pain she may have and how I try to tell her how to regulate her life so she won't hurt anymore. When I do it, it's loving care; when she does it, it's nagging. I sure need to grow here. Any suggestions?

Cancer does point out some areas of my strength, but any areas of weakness blow out like a flawed tire under pressure on a hot day. It seems that God helps us at the blow-out points so we don't get thrown into the ditch and destroyed. And cancer, more than any illness I have experienced, brings so much pressure that even the tiniest flaw or weakness—emotional, spiritual, or relational— is exposed and challenged. God's help in dealing with this process must be part of what is meant by "In all things God works for the good" (Romans 8:28). I sure am giving Him plenty to work with.

From down the road, but not far,
Your friend, Jerry

CANCER DOES POINT OUT SOME AREAS OF MY STRENGTH, BUT ANY AREAS OF WEAKNESS BLOW OUT LIKE A FLAWED TIRE UNDER PRESSURE ON A HOT DAY.

PAIN

At times it is hard to see that God is working at all, let alone working for our good. We can't see beyond the fear or pain of the immediate. Often the broader, spiritual perspective is jammed with the static intensity of the moment. But His working does not demand our attention, only His presence. He is present; therefore, He is faithfully working for our good in everything. The pain will ease. The fear will melt away, maybe just for a moment, and in that moment we will see it—His working—as evidence of His presence.

He is a very present help in trouble.

PSALM 46:1 NKJV

CHAPTER SEVEN

ANGER

The hardness of God

is kinder than the

softness of men.

C.S. LEWIS

CANCER EVOKES nearly every emotion you can think of: depression, anxiety, fear, hopelessness, victimization, and, at times, joy, hope, gratitude, love… Often, they all arrive together for a prolonged visit.

This letter is about the recurring visit of anger. For me, it was not rage or violence; it was the anger side of confusion and bewilderment.

29

Dear Ron,
From the poison cell…

I am processing some stuff. I found out that there is nothing they can do about the fractures in my pelvis. They will not heal while the chemo is going on. That is a pain management (dope) issue and I can deal with that. (They've assured me I will not become a junkie.)

The infection seems to be decreasing, and we are walking a tightrope between leaving time for it to heal and getting the radiation started as soon as possible.

I guess I am at the anger stage. I am not an "angry man," nor am I angry at anyone or anything specific. It's a little hard to describe. Rather than analyze it, I am trying to use its energy. I don't have much energy of my own, but our emotions produce energy, and if I can convert that into positive action, I can get a lot more accomplished.

Some of the anger stems from the love/hate relationship I have with the cancer. I hate it. It has rudely interrupted my life at the most inopportune time. It has brought months of excruciating pain and now promises to keep it coming. It has wrecked my already wretched body, thinned my hair, and made me look old, even to me. It interrupts my sleep, blurs my days, and demands huge blocks of my time—that makes me angry!

On the other hand, because of this diagnosis, I have entered an entirely new stage of my life. My network of friends has broadened dramatically and deepened profoundly. Our family has bonded in entirely new dimensions. I am doing more true pastoral work now than I have for ten years. My spiritual life is deepening and our marriage is richer; the gratitude levels of my life are off the chart.

My emotions seem to reside somewhere in the space between these two extremes. I am endeavoring to direct their energy to serve the love side and not the hate side. That is the challenge.

An example of the hate side occurred last night. My son and daughter are here with their spouses, and we decided to go to a movie. When the movie was over, I got up to leave, and the pain in my hips hit me in paralyzing intensity, and then my calves both cramped and I couldn't move. By the time I got out of the theater, I had attracted far too much attention, and I felt like a feeble, sick old man. The love side was that my family was not embarrassed, but loving and helpful. Having a feeble old man for a father didn't seem to bother them at all, and if not them, maybe it shouldn't bother me quite so much.

Good lessons—tough school.

From down the road, but not far,
Your friend, Jerry

I HAVE ENTERED AN ENTIRELY NEW STAGE OF MY LIFE. MY NETWORK OF FRIENDS HAS BROADENED DRAMATICALLY AND DEEPENED PROFOUNDLY.

ANGER

When someone comes, hitchhike on their joy and their hope. (But don't let the pessimists in. You don't have time to recover from them.) The energy of good emotions can be your safety net when you are sure you're falling. Take that energy into yourself and let it strengthen you.

In the dark times, when you are alone and have no defense from the encroaching fear or anger or hopelessness, remember that Jesus is comfortable with your emotions. Invite Him in to teach you how He handled those feelings. I found He not only helped me, He brought His own emotion and strength with Him.

Even though I walk through the valley of the shadow of death,
I will fear no evil, for you are with me.

PSALM 23:4

CHAPTER EIGHT

SUDDEN CHANGES

Continuity gives us roots;

change gives us branches,

letting us stretch and grow

and reach new heights.

PAULINE R. KEZER

SUDDEN CHANGES in direction can be unnerving. This cancer road is full of them. I wrote to Ron about one of mine.

The surgeon had informed us that the cancerous lymph nodes were racing around in my system with some speed. Surgery was not able to get all of them. The prospect of them metastasizing to my lungs or liver was pretty high. The last MRI was very discouraging.

Fortunately, that did not happen, but at this writing we didn't know.

33

Hi, Ron,

I am writing from my poison cell. They call it a chemotherapy suite, but I have my own term for it. Isn't it amazing that poison can cure when rightly focused? It's death to death-dealing renegade cells and releases life to the healthy ones. Sort of the way the Holy Spirit handles sin in our system. Come to think of it, His treatments are not always pleasant but they always destroy the toxic and release life.

When Barb and I got the mixed but mostly frightening report from the surgeon last Friday, we were stunned. None of the options seemed good. It had been a very long day and a draining one. I left her for a few minutes after the session. As I was returning to meet her at the truck, a thought was powerfully impressed on me. It's almost cliché, but it became very definitive *for both of us. "Get on with LIFE!" Don't mope about the future, get on with life. I told her I had made an executive decision—to just get on with life. It seemed to lift both of us. I popped a pain pill and we went to the mall to spend a gift certificate. We got home later than we intended and more tired than we believed possible, but in good spirits and rather proud of ourselves.*

It is amazing how the Holy Spirit can take a common cliché, give it life, and send it right into your spirit.

I am getting a little scattered and can no longer read my handwriting, so I will finish this later tonight.

Later…The chemo is over. I'm on the pump and doing okay.

Later still…Sorry, I got sick again.

It is now Wednesday. It is a beautiful day starting with a spectacular sunrise. (The dope wears off at 4:00 a.m.) We will be leaving soon to get the chemo pump unplugged and do a few errands in the city.

I pray you are recovering from the last round of poison. Quite a journey. I am so sorry you have to take it, but at least we can walk some of it together.

You are never far from me and constantly in my thoughts and prayers.

From down the road, but not far,
Your brother and friend, Jerry

"GET ON WITH LIFE!"

DON'T MOPE

ABOUT THE FUTURE,

GET ON WITH LIFE.

*As your days,
so shall your strength be.*

DEUTERONOMY 33:25 NKJV

SUDDEN CHANGES

We don't have a choice as to how long we will live. That is true whether we are fighting cancer or not. There are no guarantees. We do, however, have a choice as to how we will order the life we do have. That is especially important if we are battling what may be a fatal disease.

We can make the choice to live. Oh, not be alive far down the road, but today. We have today. Really, that is all any of us have. I can choose to worry and dread tomorrow, plan to die. Or I can plan to live—today. We must never miss today worrying about tomorrow; today will never come again.

Don't let the fear that cancer engenders cause you to miss the people, the sunrises, the specialness that is "today." Choose to live as many todays as come to you and live them as fully as your strength, however small, allows.

CHAPTER NINE

RECEIVING

The deeper I went into
the experience of God,
the more I found...
life in abundance.

ANDREW KLAVAN

IT IS EASY to give. It feels good and should.

Receiving is another thing altogether. I'm never sure how to respond well. I think later what I really should have said.

During my chemo treatments, I was invited to Canada to receive an honorary doctorate from a college I am associated with there. I wanted to share with you some of my feelings about receiving.

Hi, Ron,

Well, I'm back on the grill. My pump was disconnected for the weekend to allow me to go to Canada and the ceremonies without it. It was a wonderful interlude.

I was debating in my head how I should view it. There is a false humility rampant in Christian circles that says to actually enjoy this kind of thing is somehow "stealing God's glory." I was schooled in this way of thinking. But the facts they recorded about my life actually did happen as they describe.

The conflict I felt was that I really did enjoy and deeply appreciate the night. I kept thinking how unlikely it is that those opportunities would ever come to me: that I would live at a time (late '60s–'80s) that was so exceptional and blooming with doors for ministry to suffering people of all ages, but especially the young.

I found myself responding with great gratitude and awe at the life Christ has brought and is bringing to me. Help me, Ron, if I'm off base here, but I deeply enjoyed the whole affair and found myself experiencing none of the guilt religion demands. Nor do I feel a need to apologize to God for stealing any of His glory. (As if my small doing could impinge even slightly on His glory!)

Where did that stuff come from? It betrays such a shallow view of grace. It is also based on a temperamental God who must be the star of every game and get all the credit in all the post-game interviews. It's like someone complimenting a member of the San Antonio Spurs (a team I like for some reason I don't understand) whose three-point shot just won the game. Can you imagine him saying to the interviewer, "Oh, it really wasn't me. It was Tim Duncan"? Ridiculous in basketball, yet not only tolerated, but preached as Christian truth in many segments of the church.

On Saturday, I thought I could see Jesus standing and clapping with the rest of my friends. I'm His boy—and I'm being honored.

If I can't see Jesus standing with the crowd, it may be an award I have manipulated and selfishly influenced to my benefit rather than one authentically given. In that case, I doubt He would attend at all. It seems to me I must always see Him in the crowd cheering or I should not be there either.

Well, I have to go now. It took me a couple of days to finish this. I have been very sick since returning from Canada. Everything below the waist is on fire; everything above the waist is nauseous; and everything above my shoulders throbs...other than that, I'm doing okay.

I sure love you and am praying constantly for your full recovery.

From down the road, but not far,
Your friend, Jerry

I FOUND MYSELF RESPONDING WITH GREAT GRATITUDE AND AWE AT THE LIFE CHRIST HAS BROUGHT AND IS BRINGING TO ME.

RECEIVING

As life unfolds, it brings great joy and deep sorrow. Times of celebration suddenly morph into times of numbness and confusion. These conflicting events often heap up on one another.

How does Jesus view this? Where is He at these times when life collides with the unexpected, whether good and bad?

I have discovered that He accompanies me in all of life. He embraces me and eases the pain. He applauds and nods His approval at the achievement I could never have accomplished without Him. His tears mingle with mine in my sorrow.

Do not fear, for I am with you;
do not be dismayed, for I am your God.
I will strengthen you and help you;
I will uphold you with my righteous right hand.

ISAIAH 41:10

CHAPTER TEN

TOP OF THE HILL

Faithless is he

that says farewell

when the road darkens.

J.R.R. TOLKIEN

IT IS REMARKABLE how God invades us at just the perfect time. Cancer has a way of deceiving us. We feel stronger and positive. The sick levels are down (and so is the food) and some work actually is getting done. Finally, the worst is over!

Then cancer trips the lever and the gains are flushed away.

It is at those disappointing, even impossible times, that He surprises us and gives us the courage the moment demands.

41

Hi, Ron,

Last week, three weeks to the end of treatment seemed a short time. But now, two more weeks seems like an eternity. Strange how time rearranges itself.

Much of the pain has returned. The old infection is back, and the fractures have enlarged and spread. Whine, whine, whine.

On Friday, I got up at 3:30 a.m. to catch a 6:00 a.m. ferry for a 7:00 a.m. radiation treatment before leaving for a retreat in California. I was in so much pain, I had to cancel and went to an 11:00 doctor's appointment instead. The doctors were trying to help me get on a plane to go to Sacramento. After three hours of hydration and pain/nausea infusion, I made it to Old Oak Ranch at 11:30 p.m. It was an absolutely horrible day.

We were driving up the last hill before the camp. As we came around one of the sharp curves, we were suddenly and unexpectedly confronted by a full moon of huge circumference and absolutely indescribable orange in color. It was startling—it was GLORIOUS. It lay full orbed on the horizon directly ahead.

It was somehow God's benediction to the painful, impossible day. Through that momentary encounter with Him, I was able to make it to the top of the mountain and had a wonderful night's rest in a peaceful, private house reserved for me.

This morning's session was really quite remarkable, and there is little doubt that this is His assignment, accomplished totally on His strength and presence.

I guess I am telling you this to say, "We really can do this, Ron." He really is faithful. He really does weld together the horrible and the precious.

NOTE: In reviewing this letter after our phone conversation, I find I need to take my own advice and believe we can make it.

Since I wrote, the doctors have urged me to cancel all travel and interrupted the radiation/chemo regimen. I seem to be having a physical and emotional meltdown.

My daughter Christi is with me, just holding my hand. Barb began again to come to the rescue in her practical and loving way. Jamie spent the night with me. Sundar talked an hour with me on the phone. My wonderful friend Ron called and talked at length to me. Russ is coming to hang around this weekend. My point is that I think I understand that Jesus is embracing me in His love right now through all of this.

I cannot analyze where I am. I am just reaching for His hand and help for the next moment. So far, that is all I have been able to do, and, thank God, all He wants me to do.

Your call meant more than you can know.

From down the road, but not far,
Your brother and friend, Jerry

AS WE CAME AROUND ONE OF THE SHARP CURVES, WE WERE SUDDENLY AND UNEXPECTEDLY CONFRONTED BY A FULL MOON OF HUGE CIRCUMFERENCE AND ABSOLUTELY INDESCRIBABLE... IT WAS GLORIOUS.

TOP OF THE HILL

Whether it's a moon on the horizon or the gentle Christ-like embrace of those who love us, God comes to us at precisely the right time. The situation may be horrible, but His coming is precious. I really don't know how He does it, but He constantly welds these two opposites together in a remarkable braid more than strong enough to hold us together.

I don't know what He will use to braid your situation, but I know His strength will hold you together when everything seems to be falling apart.

My grace is sufficient for you.

2 CORINTHIANS 12:9

44

UPDATES

The best thing about the future

is that it comes one day at a time.

ABRAHAM LINCOLN

JERRY'S UPDATE

MY LAST LETTER was finished a year ago. Relics of the battle are still strewn around, but they are quickly being overgrown by a fragrant new life. I have begun to return to my work and my fly-fishing. Follow-up tests show that the cancer has not reoccurred.

Someone said, "Well, you're back to your old self." Actually, I don't remember my old self. I do know this self drinks deeply and gratefully of life. Friends are precious; family more precious still. I know too, whenever I see pain reflected in another's eyes, or premature hair loss hidden beneath a crooked cap, I want to gently embrace that brave fighter with hope.

SOMEONE SAID,
"WELL, YOU'RE BACK
TO YOUR OLD SELF."
ACTUALLY,
I DON'T REMEMBER
MY OLD SELF.

That is what I want these letters to be for you and those you love—a gentle embrace of love and hope.

My journey has been deepened and enriched because a wonderful friend was pressed onto the road with me. We staggered along together, but, as friendship dictates, we never lost our balance at the same time or in the same place and could steady each other a little.

However, overarching all was God's unmistakable presence. He walked in our shoes. His courage mixed with our fear, and we made it through the darkness. His strength joined our weakness, and we took the next step together. This gracious, good, and loving God was involved in every moment and inch of our journey. He is the same for you. He only asks to be invited.

The painful memories have begun to dissipate like the vapor trails of some predawn flight. They are becoming one with the clouds; wisps of brilliance in the light of a new day.

Ron's Update

IN SEPTEMBER OF 2007, I was declared "in remission." I gained all my weight back and have had four quarterly checkups as of this writing, all continuing to show remission.

During my illness, I was out of platform ministry for essentially six months, speaking once per month during the last three months of that period. Thanks to an amazing staff, I was able to be absent from all other forms of leadership except for an occasional meeting at home with a small team for thirty minutes.

Today I have resumed a full-time schedule, serving not only as the pastor of a local church but as supervisor of 43 churches in the San Francisco Bay area. Most importantly, I am able to travel again with my wife, Susan (my favorite pastime), enjoying people and places together.

NOTES

CHAPTER 1 | Proverbs 17:17 NIV

CHAPTER 2 | A quote taken from the Community Alcohol Information Program website, author unknown (www.nh-dwi.com/caip-202.htm).

CHAPTER 3 | From *The Shack* by William P. Young (Newbury Park, CA: Windblown Media, 2008), page 138.

CHAPTER 4 | Brennen Manning, interview for Christianity Today, "The Dick Staub Interview: Brennen Manning on Ruthless Trust," ChristianityToday.com 12/10/02 (www.lofitribe.com/2007/11/11/nurturing-gratitude-in-christian-community).

CHAPTER 5 | Elizabeth Scott, M.S., "The Stress Management and Health Benefits of Laughter: The Laughing Cure," About.com, updated April 22, 2008 (stress.about.com/od/stresshealth/a/laughter.htm).

CHAPTER 9 | Andrew Klavan, as told to Marvin Olasky, "Too nice for vice?" World (2-10-07), pp. 32-33.

RESOURCES

Here are some of the resources available through eastbayfellowship.org:

OUR FATHER | *a book on The Lord's Prayer*
THE NEW TESTAMENT ON CD | *the NIV read all the way through without any music or effects*
THE LOVE JOURNAL | *a daily one-year devotional guide through the New Testament, Psalms, and prophets focusing specifically on the love of God each day*
NUMEROUS TEACHING SERIES ON CD | *everything from how to resolve conflict to understanding the love of God*

And some of the resources available through www.jerrycook.org:

Books by Jerry and Barbara Cook
Teaching series—various topics on CD by Jerry Cook
Complete copies of the 18 letters sent to Ron Pinkston

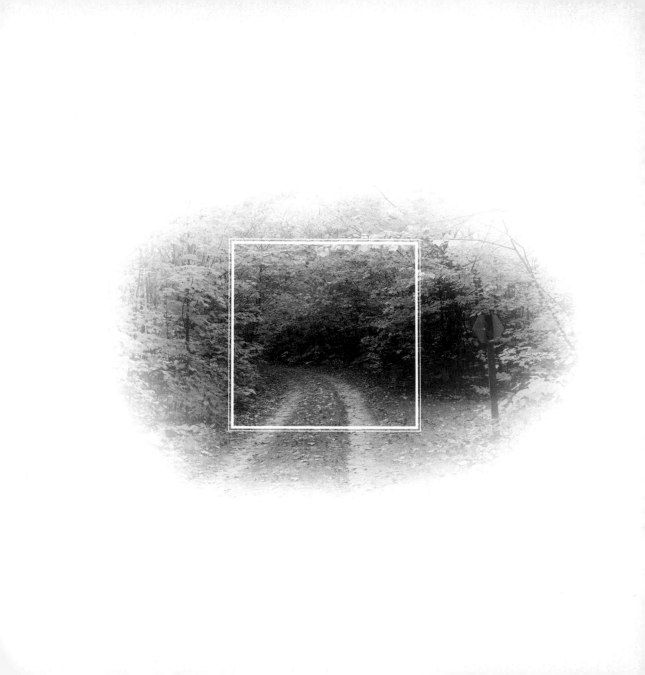